Emotional Needs

By Aaron Fields

Illustrated by: Amelia Alvin

ISBN:978-1-953962-45-4

Parenting/Caregiver Tips

By incorporating these tips, you'll be able to meet your child's emotional needs and foster a strong & healthy emotional bond with them.

When it comes to emotional needs, consider using:

- Love & affection
- Encouragement & support
- Security & stability
- Opportunities to express emotions
- Positive reinforcement & praise

Love is like a big warm hug from someone who cares about you very much. It's about feeling happy and safe when you're around them.

Affection is like giving someone a big smile to show them how much you love being around them.

Encouragement is like having someone cheer you on when you're trying your best. It's like having a cheerleader on your team, telling you that you can do it.

Support is like having someone there to help you when things get tough. They're like a superhero who always has your back.

Security is about feeling safe and protected, like having a cozy blanket to wrap around you when you feel afraid.

Stability is like having a strong tree with deep roots that will keep you steady and grounded, especially when things happen that are out of your control.

Emotions are like the different colors in a rainbow. Every color has different emotions. It's important to have a chance to talk about how you're feeling.

Whether you're happy, sad, angry, excited, or scared, expressing your emotions helps you understand yourself better and connect with others.

Positive reinforcement is like getting a gold star for doing something amazing. It shows that you're on the right track and doing a great job.

Praise is like getting a big round of applause for your hard work, making you proud, appreciated, and loved.

Parenting/Caregiver Tips

- Meeting a child's emotional needs helps them develop a strong sense of emotional intelligence, resilience and self-worth. This will allow them to manage and understand their emotions effectively and appropriately, leading to healthier relationships and better health outcomes.
- By meeting a child's emotional needs, caregivers and parents help build a strong and secure attachment. This sense of trust and security sets the foundation for healthy relationships and social interactions.
- When children feel understood and supported, they are more likely going to communicate their thoughts, feelings, and needs more effectively. This leads to more open and honest communication, which is important for creating stronger relationships and resolving problems.
- When children's emotional needs are being met, they are more likely to show positive behaviors, such as kindness, cooperation, and empathy. These children are better equipped to regulate their emotions and respond to challenges in a more positive and constructive manner.
- Neglecting a child's emotional needs can create long-term consequences on their mental health. This can lead to anxiety, depression, and low self-esteem. Believe it or not, meeting their emotional needs early on can help prevent negative outcomes.

*Always remember that providing children with emotional needs is important for their, emotional, social, and psychological development. Meeting their emotional needs will lay out the foundation for healthy relationships, positive behavior, and effective communication. This will contribute to their overall happiness and success in life.

www.ingramcontent.com/pod-product-compliance
Lightning Source LLC
LaVergne TN
LVHW010017070426
835511LV00001B/18